Giraffe

Remember Me Series

By

Caroline Norsk

Remember me I am a giraffe.

Remember me I am an African mammal.

Remember me my name means that I am a fast walker.

Remember me my mom gave birth to me while she was standing up.

Remember me I am a ruminant and I have four stomachs.

Remember me I only need to drink water once every 2-3 days.

Remember me I eat a lot.

Remember me I like to feed on grass, fruits, and shrubs.

Remember me if you see me chewing on a tree branch, it means that I am stressed.

Remember me I am very tall.

Giraffe

Remember me I have a hard time reaching the ground.

Remember me I have a long neck.

Remember me I have a brown and white coat that make me special.

Remember me I am old when the spots on my body are dark.

Remember me I always roam around wide forests.

Remember me I like to be with a herd.

Remember me I like quiet places.

Remember me I enjoy galloping.

Remember me I can live up to 25 years.

Remember me I can live up to 10 years.

Thank you.

Good Luck.